T0370515

Little Mi

My London Diary

To order additional copies of this book, contact
Toll Free +65 3165 7531 (Singapore)
Toll Free +60 3 3099 4412 (Malaysia)
www.partridgepublishing.com/singapore
orders.singapore@partridgepublishing.com

Because of the dynamic nature of the Internet, any web addresses or links contained in this book may have changed since publication and may no longer be valid. The views expressed in this work are solely those of the author and do not necessarily reflect the views of the publisher, and the publisher hereby disclaims any responsibility for them.

ISBN
ISBN: 978-1-5437-8296-7 (sc)
978-1-5437-8297-4 (hc)
978-1-5437-8295-0 (e)

Print information available on the last page.

11/28/2024

PARTRIDGE

This Diary Belong To

_____

The United Kingdom (UK) is a country that consists of England, Scotland, Wales, and Northern Ireland.

London is home to about 8.8 million people

London is the capital city of England

LONDON

UNITED KINGDOM

- ☐ ....
- ☐ ....
- ☐ ....
- ☐ ....
- ☐ ....
- ☐ ....
- ☐ ....
- ☐ ....
- ☐ ....
- ☐ ....

CHECKLIST

☐ ....

☐ ....

☐ ....

☐ ....

☐ ....

☐ ....

☐ ....

☐ ....

☐ ....

☐ ....

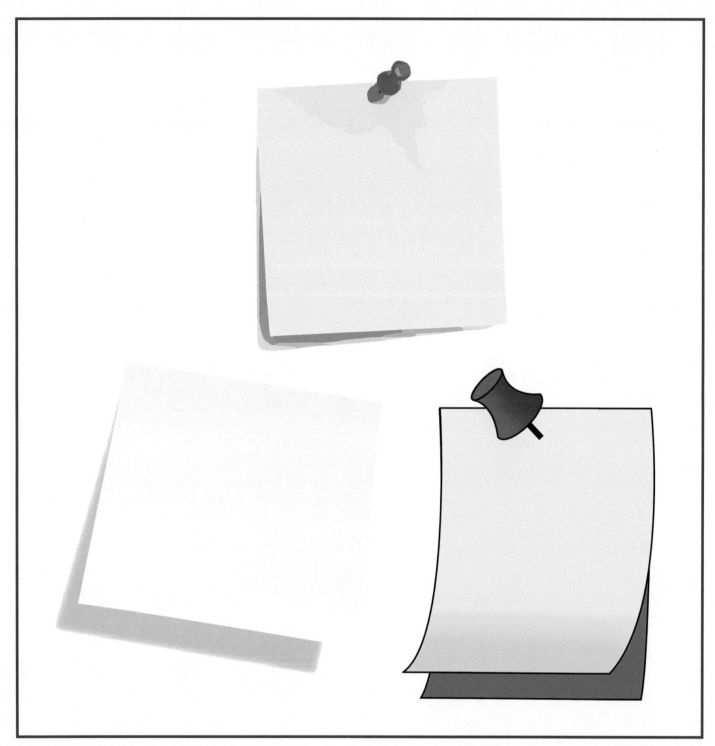

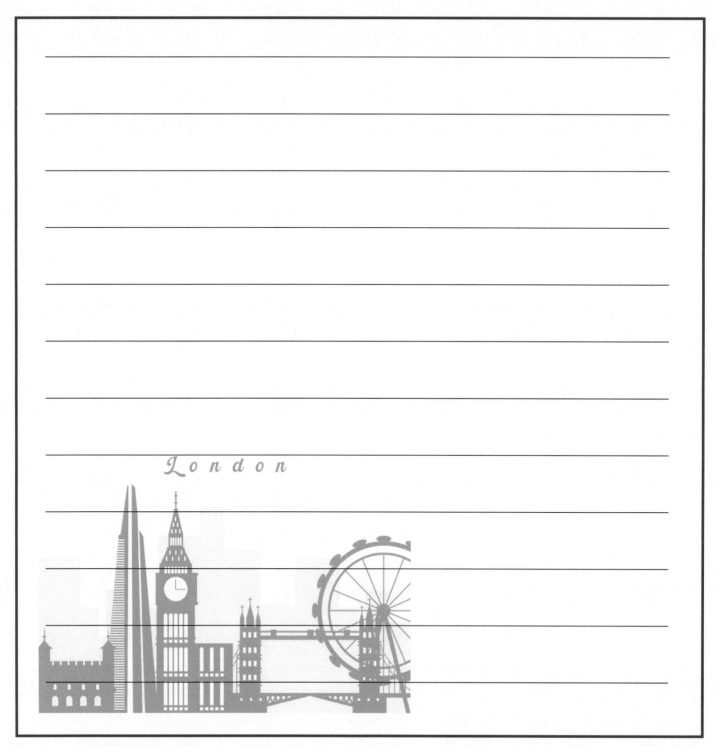

London

Tower Bridge

One of London's most famous bridges! The footpath opens up in the middle to let tall boats pass through. There's even a glass floor you can walk on to see the river below—if you're brave enough!

Many people mistake London Bridge to Tower Bridge but they're actually two different bridges!

London

Big Ben

Most people think Big Ben is the clock, but it's actually the name of the big bell inside the tower! The tower itself is called the Elizabeth Tower.

London

Black cabs in London are so roomy that an elephant could fit inside one!
Okay, maybe not a full-grown one, but it sure feels like it!

The London Eye can fit around 800 people at a time—that's like filling 11 double-decker buses! Imagine your whole school on one giant Ferris wheel.

Buckingham Palace

This is where the King lives! If you visit at the right time, you can watch the Changing of the Guards, where soldiers in red uniforms and tall black hats march around the palace.

n

Once upon a time, people used red phone booths to call their friends. Now, people just take selfies in them!

London

London

20

St. Paul's Cathedral

Its huge dome, which is one of the largest in the world!

Built in the 17th century after the Great Fire of London, St. Paul's is an iconic part of the city's skyline.

You can climb up to the Whispering Gallery inside the dome, where a whisper on one side can be heard all the way across on the other side!

London

10 Facts about London

Fun Facts

Corgi is also known as "royal dog", because Queen Elizabeth II love them.

The guards at Buckingham Palace have to stand super still, and they aren't allowed to smile—even if you make a silly face at them!

The Shard, tallest building
in UK with 72 floors

The biggest diamond, called the Cullinan Diamond, is still part of the British Crown Jewels, which are kept at the Tower of London. The Cullinan Diamond was cut into several pieces, and the largest part, known as Cullinan I or the Great Star of Africa, is on top of the royal scepter. Another large piece, Cullinan II, is set in the crown.

Things to eat

❑ Fish and chips ....

❑ ....

❑ ....

❑ Sunday Roast ....

❑ ....

❑ ....

❑ ....

❑ Shepherd's Pie ....

❑ ....

❑ ....

❑ ....

Things to do

☐ Tower of London ....

☐ ....

☐ Buckingham Palace ....

☐ ....

☐ The Harry Potter Studio ....

☐ ....

☐ London Zoo ....

☐ ....

☐ London Eye ....

☐ ....

☐ ....

London

Maze Game

Help the Dog to find the castle.

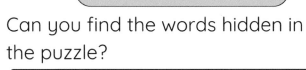

Word Search

Can you find the words hidden in the puzzle?

```
E  C  P  N  B  P  L  I  Y  T  H  S  I  P  U
X  G  T  G  Q  P  A  D  W  L  T  X  X  S  S
P  K  D  W  A  Z  Q  L  S  P  S  S  B  P  M
A  O  V  I  B  U  C  U  A  L  B  H  Z  W  O
X  C  Z  G  R  I  Z  U  O  C  B  A  G  N  X
F  Z  M  H  G  B  L  N  O  Q  E  R  D  E  I
T  X  T  R  Y  D  D  O  N  X  B  D  B  B  I
Q  C  O  W  Y  O  Z  O  E  M  I  T  D  G  Y
D  C  P  Q  N  I  X  A  T  N  B  O  J  I  H
F  Q  W  Q  X  S  P  E  X  D  O  D  F  B  U
A  Z  M  R  E  H  S  W  N  D  D  H  Z  U  J
M  K  M  S  V  X  A  K  O  J  P  F  P  K  D
B  F  I  I  B  F  V  R  D  T  U  W  K  M  X
X  W  O  E  R  E  W  O  T  M  K  O  V  U  O
B  U  C  K  I  N  G  H  A  M  G  J  S  X  B
```

London	Tower	Bridge	Big Ben	Zoo	Buckingham
Palace	Shard	St Paul	Taxi	Phone Box	Corgi

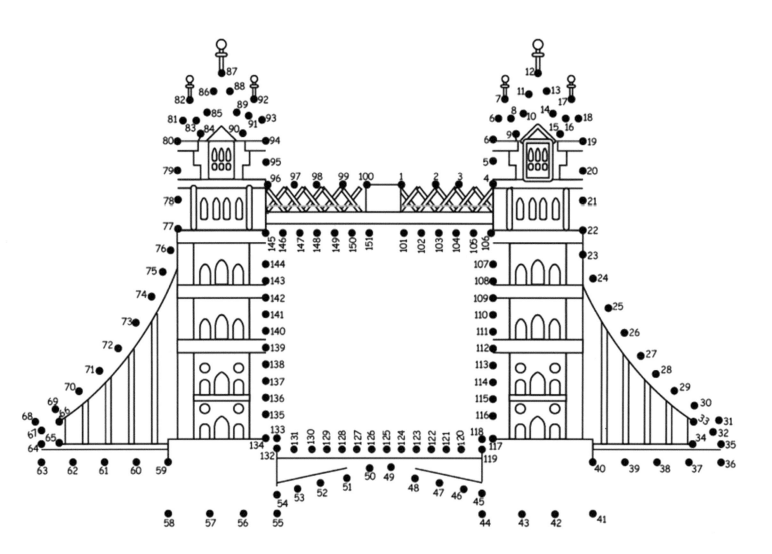

Lets help
colour
this in

London

Crossword Puzzle

ACROSS

4. What type of dog do they call them the "royal dog

6. What is the name of the tallest building UK

7. What colour hat dose the palace

9. The capital of England is

10. The name of the river running across the London city

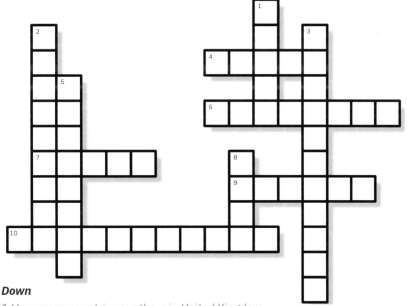

Down

1. How many countries are there in United Kingdom

2. what is the name of big ben tower

3. One famous UK Food

5. What is the name of the Diamond on Kings Crown call

8. The colour of United Kingdom flag is White, Red and which colour

London

Printed in the United States
by Baker & Taylor Publisher Services